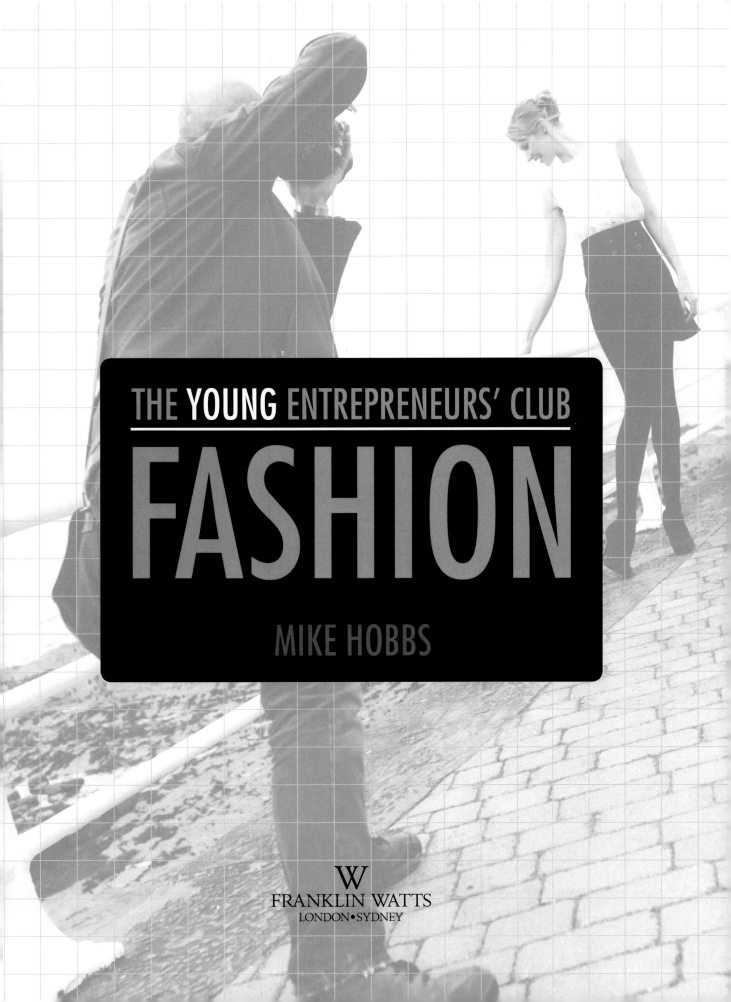

# THE YOUNG ENTREPRENEURS' CLUB

# FASHION

## MIKE HOBBS

W
FRANKLIN WATTS
LONDON • SYDNEY

Series Editor: Paul Rockett
Consultant: David Gray
Design: Simon Burrough
Picture Research: Diana Morris

Dewey number: 338.4'774692

ISBN: 978 1 4451 3926 5

Printed in China

Franklin Watts is a division of
Hachette Children's Books,
an Hachette UK company.

www.hachette.co.uk

# CONTENTS

# Fashion highlights

## The business of fashion

What do we mean by the fashion business? There's quite a difference between the glamorous fashion shows we read about in magazines and the clothes shops in your local town. But everyone who works for a large designer label or a small shop is a part of the fashion world.

Fashion is an exciting business, and the fashion world revolves around a series of fashion weeks. This is where models show off the clothes of the top designers on the catwalks. The four major centres of this fashion world are:
- New York City
- London
- Milan
- Paris.

Each city hosts a fashion week twice a year for women's clothing. These are held in February and March for the Autumn and Winter Collections, and in September and October for the following year's Spring and Summer Collections. Gaps between these dates allow time for buyers to order the clothes for their shops. This also allows time for the fashion media to have their say. Of course, there are many other fashion shows in other cities around the globe.

## Facts:

According to one estimate, the global clothing industry had reached a value of over US$1,780 billion (£1,138 billion) by the end of 2010.

Roughly 80% of clothes worn are made from non-organic products.

About 12 billion pounds of textile clothing each year will end up as landfill. Half of these clothes are polyester and are therefore non-biodegradable.

Vintage clothes are those made between 1920 and 1960. After 1960, they're described as retro.

## Fashion jobs

Apart from being a designer or a model, there are plenty of other ways you can make your mark. You could be a fashion reporter, a photographer, a stylist, a dresser, a make-up artist or run a boutique. It's not necessary to be in high fashion to make a very good living.

Like all the creative industries, there is very strong competition. You are only as good as your last piece of work and there are many people pushing to take your place. However, it is possible to build a long career in fashion. One secret is to become an entrepreneur.

**CHALLENGE**

Write a list of all the different areas of the fashion industry you can think of. List them with the one that interests you most at the top.

# Young Entrepreneurs

## Send the Trend

Mariah Chase and Divya Gugnani (bottom), are both passionate about fashion. This is a passion that drives the success of their company, Send the Trend.

Send the Trend is an online shop selling and advising on fashion accessories. The user takes a style survey and accessories are displayed based on what they can afford.

Divya used to go to shops and have personal shoppers help her find the clothes that she wanted. She noticed that this was increasingly expensive and so set about thinking of a way to offer a cheaper alternative. Send the Trend looks to offer the experience of a personal shopper by being able to recommend items suited to the user.

The company has over 50,000 subscribers and is still growing. The people that run the company have created a successful business out of doing what they love – checking out the latest fashions and researching new accessories!

**YOUR THOUGHTS**

What parts of the fashion industry does Send the Trend cover?

# What makes a successful entrepreneur?

## Risk-taking

Entrepreneurs are risk takers who see business opportunities where others don't. A successful entrepreneur will make a profit by investing time, money and energy into a project. Often in the fashion world, the creative and business ideas come from the same person.

## What does a fashion entrepreneur do?

He or she spots a gap in the market, in other words has an idea for something that no-one else is providing, and goes ahead and turns that idea into a reality. These ideas may come from personal experience, and knowing what they're good at doing. They may also come from seeing things that work well. Anything can spark inspiration. Do you have some ideas that you'd love to take forward? What are you interested in making or doing?

You've got to have talent of your own and you must have confidence in yourself. You'll have to work very hard if you want to succeed. But you'll find a combination of natural flair, attention to detail and an ability to keep going can take you a very long way.

**CHALLENGE**

**Look at your list of areas within the fashion industry, and focus on the ones that interest you most. Can you think of any ways you could create a business around these areas? Try and write down at least two ideas.**

## Inspiring Entrepreneur

### Ralph Lauren

One great example of an entrepreneurial wizard is Ralph Lauren (left). The founder of Polo turned a small business selling ties into one of the fashion world's success stories. He worked for a tie company in the 1960s. He noticed that wide ties were coming into fashion and so started designing his own versions to sell. Deciding to expand his range and go solo, he launched his company in 1968 with a $50,000 loan.

It was a good decision. He received an award for his 1970 menswear collection, and within two years, his famous Polo label was first used on designer women's clothing. When the US shop Bloomingdale's asked him to redesign some of his range he refused, and sure enough his fashion sense was right, and the shop soon stocked his clothes. Throughout his career he has shown an instinct for fashion and a confidence to stick by his own decisions. Now he has 35 boutiques in the US and around the world, and is estimated to be worth $6 billion.

**YOUR THOUGHTS**

What do you think is the most important thing you can learn from famous fashion entrepreneurs, such as Ralph Lauren?

# Trying out your ideas

## What will work?

OK, so you've got a few ideas, but are they ones that will be successful? Do they have broad appeal, or is it just your own taste in fashion?

Let's say you've had an idea for making a new style of women's jacket, one that would be good for wearing both at work and out in the evening. A good start might be to make one or two versions of the jacket, and give them to friends or relations to try out. Make sure that they wear them at least once on a night out and once to work.

A few days later, meet up with them and see what they have to say about the jackets. Did they feel comfortable at all times? This is obviously a must. Was it suitable in both situations? This test might give you some feedback. You should also take special notice of any comments or enquiries they received from other people while they were trying out your jackets.

**CHALLENGE**

If you wanted to enter the fashion industry as a stylist or photographer, how might you test these skills or results? Who might you want to get feedback from?

# Young Entrepreneur
## TOMS

Blake Mycoskie (below) soon knew his shoes were potential winners. He had the idea while he was travelling around South America on holiday, and could see how effective they already were. His designs were based on shoes worn by Argentinian farmers for many years, so the product was tried and tested. He knew there was a need because of the serious health risks of swollen feet with over 1 billion people at risk of being affected. His canvas or cotton fabric shoes with rubber soles would help to prevent this.

He launched TOMS Shoes (from the 'tomorrow' in their slogan, 'Shoes for Tomorrow Project') in 2006 from Arlington, Texas. They were an immediate hit, and he received the People's Design Award in 2007. One of the reasons is that Blake gives away a pair of shoes to poor people for each pair sold – he calls this 'One For One'. They have built sales each year and 1,000,000 had been sold by 2010. Now TOMS has moved into selling other types of shoes, clothing and glasses, also using the 'One For One' initiative.

**YOUR THOUGHTS**

How did Blake know that the shoes were 'tried and tested'? If he hadn't been aware of this, what could he have done to test the shoes?

# Research your market

## What's out there?

The fashion industry is incredibly tough. Are there enough people around who are going to buy your clothes, your shoes or your hats? How many people are likely to visit your shop? Are you going to sell online? You must research your potential market.

Having tested your product, you've now got to do some classic market research to find your answers, and there are two main types:

**Primary research** involves collecting and using new information. For this you may want to have a questionnaire to give to people in the street.

**Secondary research** means collecting and using existing information, from the library, magazines and on the Internet. You might be able to find out about fashion trends.

**Magazines could prove a good source of secondary research.**

CHALLENGE

Can you think of any unusual, inexpensive ways to research your market? What questions could you ask? What information should you be looking for in fashion magazines?

**YOUR THOUGHTS**

By seeing what was popular at her fashion shop, was Mich completing primary or secondary research?

# Young Entrepreneur
## Mich Dulce

This award-winning milliner set about researching and creating a market for her hats in an unusual way. Mich sings with a rock band and has appeared on the Filipino version of *Big Brother*. These have made her better known to a wider public and have helped establish a fan-base.  However, she also has a background in fashion.

She had previously attended the College of Fashion at Central St Martins School of Art in London, and then studied merchandise planning at the Fashion Institute of Technology in New York. In 2005, she opened the shop Store for All Seasons with a friend. This is a fashion shop and it gave her the opportunity to research what styles and clothes people wanted. In speaking to customers she discovered that there was a gap in the market for one-off individual hats – and she has set about filling it successfully.

In 2007, she received Streetwear Fashion Designer of the Year, at the MEGA awards; and in 2010, she got the prestigious Fashion IYCE Award at London Fashion Week. In addition to her famous hats, Mich also makes corsets and bridal gowns.

# Finding start-up funds

## Getting started

As your business idea develops, you will need to find money to cover your start-up costs. The amount you need can depend on the size of your idea. You may even have enough of your own money, but you might need to ask friends, relatives or others. You may even be able to get a bank loan.

There are also some charitable bodies that give out grants to encourage businesses. You might be eligible for a government grant. It's worth investigating these, and also companies within the fashion industry that may want to invest when they see your product.

If you involve other people, they become your backers. They will need some clear and realistic financial plans to show that you've got a chance of success. Work out all the costs involved in your product and predict your sales to show when they will receive a financial return.

**CHALLENGE**

You are looking to manufacture hair accessories. You know your manufacturing costs will be steady throughout the year, and you expect sales to grow by 5% each month. Put this information onto a chart that you might use to show a backer.

# Young Entrepreneur
## Fifth & Brannan

Based in San Francisco, Kate Wintrode is the founder and head designer of Fifth & Brannan, a men's shirt business. Her idea was that she would provide quality, timeless men's clothing with modern tailoring, offering more texture, greater colour patterns, and many personal touches.

But, like many, she needed funds to begin her project. She turned to a website called Kickstarter. Here you can explain your business venture in a short video and give details of what investors will get in return. Kate set a target of $13,000 to launch her collection. She successfully reached this sum with investments made through the site. As a result, her premiere shirt collection for Autumn/Winter 2011 was launched. Sales have been so good that Kate's business is now expanding into offering a greater range of menswear.

**YOUR THOUGHTS**

How is recording a video and putting it on a website a good way to attract investors?

# Developing your product

## Vital development

You've tested your product, researched your market and found some money to get you going. But there's still a lot to do before you can actually sell your product or provide your service. This can be difficult to take because you know how fast tastes in fashion change, and you're keen to move swiftly.

However, it's very important to think about the following questions. If you're producing an item of clothing, what materials and fabrics will be used? What methods will you use to make your designs? How and where will they be stored? If you're providing a service, what's needed to make it the best quality? These can all affect the success of your business.

## Setting standards

Be very careful about choosing between quality and cost. Within your budget, you should always set the standards of quality that you want, especially for your clothes. Make sure your clothes stay above this standard. Don't be tempted to use cheaper materials if they do not suit your designs. In fashion, your reputation is vital and must not suffer through poor quality. At a later stage, you can always try to cut back costs.

**CHALLENGE**

You're designing some gloves. Write down three ways in which you can develop them, always keeping them within the top-quality range.

# Young Entrepreneurs
## ModCloth

Susan Koger's love for vintage and retro clothing started when she was in high school. She would spend her spare time shopping around for unique items of old clothing. She met Eric at college (both pictured above), and then married him. Together they began their online clothing shop ModCloth in 2006, selling all the amazing clothes that Susan had collected. Soon the company branched out into selling new designs. So far, so normal. Using blogs, Twitter, Facebook and other social media networks, such as Chictopia, customers were able to give feedback.

What is different is where they invite their customers to recommend materials for quality and also make suggestions on product lines. The Kogers call this their 'Be the Buyer' initiative. It is all part of Susan's plan to change the fashion industry. She wants customers to have an important say in product quality and choice. ModCloth has extended into accessories and décor, and has grown steadily so it now has 100 employees.

**YOUR THOUGHTS**

What are the benefits of getting the customer to advise on materials?

# Will it wear well?

## Designing to last

Well, it may look great, but will it stand up to the pressures of everyday wear? Even if you're designing haute couture (high quality fashion) as opposed to ready-to-wear, it still has to be durable. There's a good way to find out. Get some friends to wear your clothes or wear them yourself. This is another important side of market research known as product testing or product trialling.

It may look great on the catwalk, but will it wear well in the street?

**CHALLENGE** You've designed and manufactured a pair of walking shoes. How will you test them? Write out a list of the different ways and environments these may need to be trialled in.

The difference between this stage of testing and that described on page 12 is that then you were testing a prototype. Now you're testing the final product or service. If it's an item of clothing you will also be able to find out how it alters in shape or feel after washing or dry-cleaning. These may not seem vital for sales but are for after-sales service.

One of the advantages of having so many stages in the development process is that it gives you a chance to react to any changes in fashion. It also gives you yet another chance to put things right if you discover any problems.

# Young Entrepreneur
## Masala Tee

Masala Tee is an online T-shirt sales company with an Indian slant. Besson Noelline and Sheikha Mattar-Jacob (above) set up the Masala Tee company in New Delhi, India in May 2009 to sell their T-shirts. Masala is the Hindi word for spice, and they decided to trade on the world's love for Indian tea and spices. The clothing is made out of sustainable fabrics from ethically sound factories. They are 100% organic cotton, environmentally friendly and comfortable.

The T-shirts are in four styles: Masala Tee Jewel for women (embedded with Swarovski stones), Urban for men with some edgier designs, Sugarcube for children and the ethnic Blooming range (based on tea flavours!). Because the T-shirts are made in different centres and need to travel around the world, they have to ensure they are robust (even the jewelled ones). They have brought in a system of quality control, so all T-shirts are tested to see they meet high standards and will last properly. Masala Tee is now offering scarves and accessories to boost sales to its customers.

**YOUR THOUGHTS**

How important do you think long life is for fashion items such as T-shirts?

# Know your competition

## Research your rivals

**If you're opening a shop, will you be competing with other high street outlets?**

It's highly unlikely that your idea is going to be on its own in the market. Who are you going to be up against? Who are your competitors? This is the final part of your research and is just as important as the others. It really is true that the more you research, the more chance you will have to succeed.

You've probably noticed some competitors already. Now is the time to study them closely. You don't have to do it all yourself.

Ask your friends and family to keep their eyes and ears open and let you know about any rivals who might affect your success.

Look at what they do well and take special notice of what they don't. Also, keep thinking about what the next fashion trends are likely to be, and whether your rivals are able to respond. If not, can you take the advantage and gain sales?

**CHALLENGE**

**What fashion trends can you see coming in the next year? Think about how fashion has changed over the last two years.**

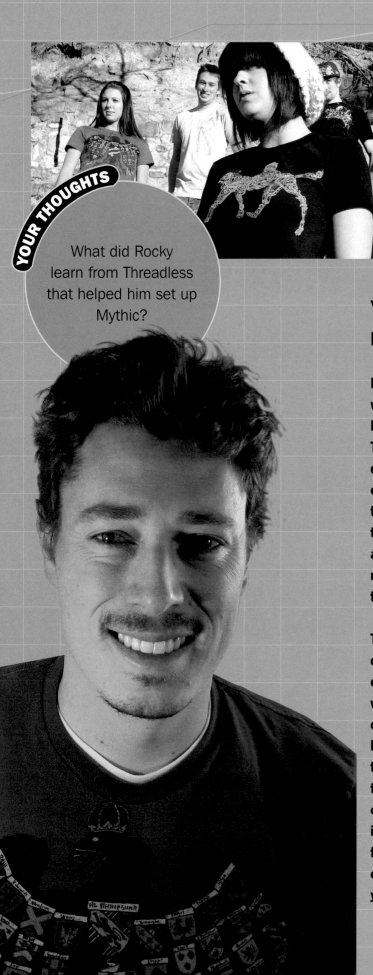

**YOUR THOUGHTS**

What did Rocky learn from Threadless that helped him set up Mythic?

## Young Entrepreneur
### Mythic

Rocky Davies (left) had a good idea of what his competition was going to be, as he'd previously done some work for them. Threadless is a company that sells T-shirts with designs submitted through a weekly online competition. Having submitted designs for their public vote, Rocky was able to gain exposure and learn about what makes a good T-shirt. This inspired him to set up a rival T-shirt label called Mythic, selling T-shirts that he has designed.

Threadless is one of the biggest T-shirt sites on the market, over 700 designs competing each week to be made into T-shirts. It has a wide reach through word-of-mouth and a buzz on the Internet other companies crave. This kind of exposure is what Rocky sees as being the most important factor for his company to compete and survive. As he says: "You can have the coolest shirts on the Web, but if nobody knows about them, the company fails. On the other hand, you can have all the exposure in the world but if your shirts suck, you'll never really catch on."

# Budget for success

## Budgeting and cash flow

If your products are to show true profit you'll have to make sure you're adding in all the costs of your venture, however unrelated they may seem. You'll have to include the costs of transport, electricity and storage, as well as the costs of making and selling your product.

As soon as you've found the money to develop your plans, begin working out a proper budget. Include all the costs you'll have to pay and be realistic about your likely sales. Your profit is the money you bring in less your costs. Your venture must be profitable. It won't matter how good your idea is if you can't make money on it.

You must not only make a tidy profit but also make sure there is a regular flow of cash into the business. This can be almost as hard to do, but it is crucial for entrepreneurs who regularly have to pay out for costs such as materials and electricity. People in the fashion industry would like to depend on money from the buying public being reliable, but we all know they can sometimes be fickle!

**CHALLENGE**

You have set up a portable shoe repair business, whereby you travel by bike around the city fixing and polishing shoes. You don't have to pay for premises, but your bike is insured against theft or damage. Write out a list of all the other things that you pay for.

# Young Entrepreneur
## Chapar

In London in September 2013, Sam Middleton set up Chapar, his business designed to solve styling problems for men who don't like to shop, even though he had always sworn he didn't want to work in the city. But of course he was smart enough to base himself where his main market lives. He reckons that the breakthrough moment for him was when a customer told him that he would never set foot inside a shop again.

Although maybe it is the way he has planned for the company's success that is even more notable. Methodically overcoming any doubts, Sam has gone about seeking funding for Chapar in a traditional, professional way. He has rapidly brought in enough funds from a not only to hire 10 experienced stylists, but to make it realistic that the company was profitable by the end of 2014.

His men's styling and shopping service sends out handpicked clothes to customers who only pay for what they choose – and send the rest back without charge. Turnover is anticipated to exceed £1 million in the first trading year.

**YOUR THOUGHTS**

How has Sam's company benefited from his attention to financial planning and detail?

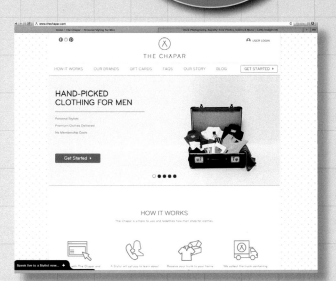

# Gathering support

## Forming a team

Working in the fashion industry will require a lot of your time and attention. You may struggle to do everything and so you might need other people's input. This can be extremely valuable if they have strengths in areas of business that you lack. Think about getting a good team together.

Your business may need people to take on roles about which you know little, such as web design or dressmaking. You'll need to think about the skills the person needs to have to fill these roles as well as where you will find them. You could advertise, go through an agency or find someone through a friend. You must be sure that they can do the job and so you should interview them thoroughly. Whoever you choose, it's best to make sure that they share your belief in and enthusiasm for your idea. A shared fashion sense is likely to be essential!

**Your team may range from people sewing your products to those selling them.**

**CHALLENGE**
**You are interviewing people for the role of stylist for your business. Write out the questions you'll need to ask them.**

# Young Entrepreneur
## Péro

Aneeth Arora is the founder of Péro. Péro means 'to wear' in Marwari, the local language of Rajasthan in India. Aneetha makes women's clothes, menswear and clothing for children. Her label sells her designs through 60 shops in 15 countries. As well as showing her women's fashion designs in Delhi, Aneeth also takes part in the fashion weeks in New York, Milan and Paris. Her company won the British Council Young Fashion Entrepreneur of the Year award for 2011.

Aneetha was a textile graduate from the National Institute of Design, Ahmedabad and a fashion graduate from India's National Institute of Fashion Technology. Inspired by the local people, Aneeth set out to design clothes that would feel natural anywhere in the world yet still make people think of India. She uses at least 80 craftspeople throughout India to make her designs. Aneeth decided to handle the recruitment of every one of those dressmakers and craftspeople personally, because ensuring they have the right skills is so important for her business.

**YOUR THOUGHTS**

What would happen to Aneeth's products had she employed people with the wrong skills?

# Leading from the front

## Leadership and decision-making

You'll need to be decisive to keep one step ahead of fashion trends. One of the things you must find time for is sufficient space for thinking when you're making these vital decisions. So, you'll need to sharpen your problem-solving skills. You'll also need to learn to manage your time effectively. Leaders need time to make decisions, and one of your hardest tasks will be to find some breathing space. You'll need to make sure you do only what is essential, and not what others think you should do.

On the other hand, although all the major decisions are up to you, you need to be able to listen to advice from all your team – on what to make next, for instance. Use their experience: that's what you hired them for, after all. Leadership also involves inspiring others, and people are more likely to follow your direction if they feel they are contributing. Personal relationships are very important in fashion.

**Before finding his own success as a leader in women's fashion, Yves Saint Laurent (right) was managed and inspired by the equally successful Christian Dior.**

It's also worth reading up about how the great fashion entrepreneurs became successful. There are always useful tips you can pick up from their stories about how they made the important decisions that put them on the path to fortune.

**CHALLENGE**

**What do you think is the best way to manage your time? State two ways of keeping control.**

# Young Entrepreneur
## American Apparel

**YOUR THOUGHTS**

Do you think it's better to approach your team in a formal business manner or more casually, like Dov? Why?

American Apparel from Los Angeles has been one of fashion's big success stories and the leadership style of Canadian founder Dov Charney (left) is both controversial and highly effective. He calls himself a 'contrarian' which means he does the opposite of everyone else. His personal involvement in the making of his company's advertisements and his relaxed behaviour and language have been criticised. An entrepreneur from his schooldays, he admits his method is almost the opposite of other business leaders, but claims it promotes creativity. He also believes in fair treatment of workers and insists on paying a fair wage. This is done not out of kindness, but because he believes it is better for business.

More conventionally, he makes all the decisions on the hiring of creative people and the important decisions on product development. He brought in an idea of team manufacturing where the most skilled designers work on the most profitable orders. There has been some controversy about what he does, but it works. He sold American Apparel for $360 million in 2006 in order to take it public, and is now President and CEO. In 2008, he was Retailer of the Year and, among many other awards, has also been Fashion Guild's Man of the Year.

# Work out a marketing plan

## Stirring the marketing mix

Now decide what your marketing plan is going to be. Simply put, this means working out how you can encourage as many people as possible to go out and buy your great new product. So much happens so fast in fashion, you must plan carefully.

The point of a marketing plan is to match the strengths of your product to the needs of your target market. For example, if your customers are most interested in buying high-quality jeans, you need to ensure your marketing strategy highlights your jeans' quality above all else.

## The four Ps

Once you've decided on your plan, you need to put it into action. To do this, it's often helpful to think of the four Ps:
**Product:** What your product offers and what sets it apart from its competition. For example, Croc shoes are light and waterproof – perfect for the beach.

**Price:** What your customers will be prepared to pay for the product.
**Place:** Where you are going to sell your product – in shops, supermarkets, online or all three.
**Promotion:** How to reach your market most effectively. This can include advertising, public relations (PR), sales promotions and by, let's hope, creating a brand.

# Young Entrepreneur

## Johnny Cupcakes

Johnny Cupcakes is a cult brand of clothing launched in 2001 by Johnny Earle (below) in Massachusetts, USA. It uses cupcakes as its main logo, incorporating them into quirky, eye-catching designs. Johnny launched the brand at age 17 with the best possible kind of visible promotion – he wore them himself (often onstage with his band). Friends saw his designs and wanted to buy their own versions, and Johnny was soon swamped with demand, including offers from some big chain stores.

But he decided that a lot of his brand's appeal was that it was quirky and different, not mass-market. He chose to keep his operation small and personal, starting off selling his clothes online and through selected, high-quality shops. In 2005, he opened his own bakery-inspired shop in his hometown, Hull, USA, where cupcakes are given away with the clothes. There are now others in Boston, Los Angeles and London. He was voted USA's No.1 Entrepreneur in 2008.

**YOUR THOUGHTS**

How has Johnny Earle promoted his product?

# Spreading the word

## Getting people's attention

It is vital that people know about your product. Are your target customers aware of what you're doing? If you've done your research, you'll know who is your target market. Now you must find the best ways to reach it.

Plan your advertising campaign, and support it with some promotional work. Good public relations (PR) is essential in fashion, especially if your advertising is unlikely to be as big as your larger rivals.

Advertising is usually paid for and aims to get your product in the right media, either in print or online, to grab your customers' attention. A new fashion venture can be publicised by holding a launch event or promotion.

But it may be possible to get free publicity. For example, if you're setting up a jewellery business, you might start a blog, use word of mouth or get reviewed in the local media, by getting someone well-known to wear a piece.

**CHALLENGE**

You're setting up a clothes-swap website. Your target market is students. How best can you draw their attention to your site? Write out three different ways.

# Young Entrepreneur

## Lora Leedham

Jewellery designer Lora Leedham (below) from Birmingham, England, knew what she wanted to do from the first moment of a college lecture on making jewellery. When she started in 2006, Lora couldn't afford to do any marketing so she relied on word-of-mouth to get her name and designs known, selling her first designs to friends and family at parties and events. Sales began to happen – slowly.

But Lora's big break came when she seized the initiative and wrote to Camilla, the Duchess of Cornwall (wife of the Prince of Wales). Lora asked the Duchess whether she could design a piece of jewellery for her to wear. Camilla accepted and wore Lora's necklace at the highly publicised 30th anniversary celebrations of the Prince's Trust. Suddenly Lora's necklace was in all the celebrity magazines, followed by features in *Grazia* and *Vogue* and appearances on TV. Within a year, Lora was able to set up her own shop, and her reputation and success continue to grow.

**YOUR THOUGHTS**

Why was the Duchess of Cornwall a good person for Lora to have approached?

# The big day

## Launch time

At last, you're ready. It's all been building up to this. Spare no effort to make sure your launch is as successful as possible. The fashion world is always looking for something new. This is your advantage, so make the most of it!

You must get the publicity machine working overtime. Social media networks must be buzzing with the date you've set. In the same way, any advertising you do must be centred around the launch day. And, of course, PR must do the same thing. You're looking for maximum exposure.

Any other promotions should either concentrate on the day or run from the day of the launch for a short time. This is when you have a great chance to get people to try or experience your product. Will you launch with an event which will allow people to experience your service or goods? Could you offer a special price without putting your long-term plans at risk?

**CHALLENGE**

It's summer and you're launching a range of beachwear. You want to have a party and have a catwalk show, however you don't have enough money left for a venue. What do you do?

# Young Entrepreneur
## Prodiga

Jennifer Levenston (above) did everything she could to make sure her launch was a success. She left Leeds Art College in the UK at 19, with a clear idea of what she wanted to do. She was going to design high quality, fashionable work clothes for women. The name she chose was a clue: *Prodiga* means 'lavish' in Italian. Her clothes would look expensive but would be affordable.

Her research suggested that although selling these clothes might seem to be difficult in a recession, there was still a big need for them. Still she had to get a lot of things right. Her plan was to launch in 2010 for her Spring/Summer Collection 2011. She contacted the Garden of the Year award winners to see if she could do the photoshoot there. By placing her clothes within beautiful gardens, the clothes looked even more beautiful. This was the first time that people were able to see these clothes and so it was incredibly important that they looked just right to make the best impact.

**YOUR THOUGHTS**

Why was it important for Jennifer to find the right location in which to photograph her new collection?

# Don't rest – could you do better?

## Running your business

Now you've launched, are you sure that all the decisions you took earlier are right? Could you be getting your materials at a better price? Are you selling through the right outlets? It's no problem if you want to change a few things.

Once you've launched, things don't stop there. If anything, they get even harder. You are now running a daily business and also have to plan for future sales.

You have to watch things like a hawk at the start (not a bad idea for your entire business career in fact). From the very first day, check all the sales figures regularly and carefully. You also have to see that cash flow is good. Make sure that all the money from sales is coming into the business and that enough is in the bank to cover day-to-day expenses.

**CHALLENGE**

Your business is producing a range of waterproof jackets, which you are marketing for large children. Name one idea for bringing down costs, and one for increasing sales.

# Young Entrepreneur
## Paperfeet

Sometimes, running your business properly demands a fast decision that makes you more profitable, as well as helping the planet. Jimmy Tomcszak (right) thought quickly when he found a potential source for the materials for his eco-friendly shoes. He graduated from the University of Michigan in Ann Arbor, USA, in 2010. At the same time he formed his company, Tombolo, which now makes goods out of materials that would otherwise end up in landfill sites, where they would be a problem for the environment.

It produces Paperfeet, the first sandals in the world made from advertising billboard material. Jimmy discovered this material when he was working on a building project and didn't have enough money for a proper roof. The contractor said that billboard vinyl did the trick, and Jimmy found it would be ideal for the prototype shoes that he had been working on at the same time. He scrapped his original plans, focused on the new material, and the rest is history. His company has been named as one of 100 Brilliant Companies by *Entrepreneur Magazine*.

**YOUR THOUGHTS**

Why was having the right material important for Paperfeet?

# Putting things right

## Reacting fast

So, it's all gone well, but you're not fully satisfied with all that's happening. Now is the time to put it right. Even big problems can be solved if necessary – it's never too late. Keep trying different approaches until you've got everything just how you want it.

And there will be problems. This is the real world, and nobody expects perfection. A vital person falls ill, there's a power cut affecting your online sales, a van breaks down or there's a strike in your neighbourhood. It's really hard in such a fast-moving business as fashion, but you have to be realistic. Some things are beyond your control: just try to get round them as best you can.

One of the important things to remember is you must always let your customers know if there are going to be any delays or changes to the plan. A simple message on your website, or by phone, text or email could buy you a lot of good will and save you a lot of bother later.

**CHALLENGE**

Your new T-shirts are due to be launched at a trade fair, but you've just heard your lorry is stuck in a traffic jam on the motorway. What can you do to help?

# Young Entrepreneur
## Missy La La's

Kirsten Dunnett (below) from Glenrothes in Scotland decided to open a fashion boutique in nearby Dundee. She had noticed that there was no funky clothes shop there for young women, so she thought she'd fill the gap in the market. Her research was proved right – opening in 2008 with a £5,000 loan from the Prince's Trust (a charitable fund), her boutique has been very successful.

But that doesn't mean there haven't been problems. She had studied the Business of Fashion at college in Kirkcaldy but still found several things she needed to find out about when she opened the shop. As a young woman, she had to learn to cope with older, more experienced fashion salesmen hoping to pull the wool over her eyes. She needed to learn about accountancy and tax issues, often asking her mother for advice. She had to grasp the importance of keeping Missy La La's clean and tidy. All little things, maybe, but they can soon add up! Now she's coping, almost single-handed, and going from strength to strength.

**YOUR THOUGHTS**

What features of business did Kirsten have to learn quickly in order to stay successful?

# Next steps

## Keep moving

Congratulations! Your efforts have been such a hit that you'll soon have a well-known brand on your hands. So right now is the time to be thinking about how and where you can start extending your fashion range. Don't be afraid to think big now you know how it's done. Within reason, of course: remember you can't do everything at once!

Above all, don't stand still. Fashion is constantly on the move, and you must make sure you're always planning what you're going to do next.

**You could raise your profile, perhaps with shop displays or celebrity endorsements.**

## Expand

Look for new products that you know your loyal customers will also want to buy. If they trust your taste in men's shirts, for instance, they are likely also to trust your taste in men's suits. It makes sense to use your established network of customers rather than trying to develop a new one straightaway. Let the larger network grow gradually, and you'll be on the way to your next success.

**CHALLENGE**

**You launched a fashion magazine focusing on accessories. It has been a great success. Suggest three things that you might want to do next.**

# Young Entrepreneurs
## Pinzat

Sam and Dolca from Barcelona, Spain, met at art college with a shared love of bikes, bags and graffiti. In setting up Pinzat (meaning 'pegged') they were able to combine all of these elements. They began creating bags suitable for cycling, from 100% recycled material. Each bag has its own unique design, created by one of their artists and are all hand sewn with a double seam, ensuring great durability for a long life.

The bags proved a great success. Customers loved the designs and material, so they felt encouraged to extend their range and have gone on to produce lap-top and iPad cases, wallets and cycle straps. By not standing still they have kept the business fresh and interesting. The development of products and ideas has seen the company grow in success.

**YOUR THOUGHTS**

How else could Pinzat develop their product range or business?

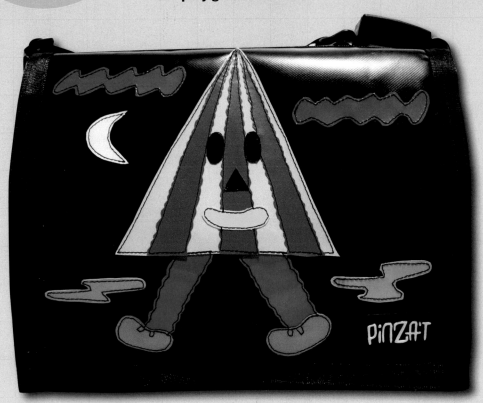

# Glossary

**advertising** Images and text that interest people in your product or business.

**backers** People who lend you money to help you start your business.

**brand** A characteristic or trademark that identifies a product.

**broad appeal** The idea or belief that your product will be attractive to many people.

**budget** The amount of money you expect to spend and receive.

**cash flow** The money coming in and going out.

**competitors** Everyone who is competing with you to sell to consumers.

**costs** Everything you must spend to make sales.

**cult brand** An article of fashion known and loved by a few.

**entrepreneur** Someone who takes a financial risk in order to make a profit.

**exposure** The amount of media coverage your product or business receives.

**fashion range** All the different types of product that you make.

**fashion trends** What is happening at the moment and is likely to happen in the future.

**feedback** Comments on what you've said, made or done.

**financial plans** Estimates of how much money you need and how much you'll make.

**financial return** How much money you get back from your investment.

**inspiration** Anything or anyone giving you ideas or self-belief.

**invest** Put money into a business.

**launch** The moment you open your business or start selling your product.

**logo** A memorable image that represents your company or business.

**marketing mix** The things you must do to market your goods.

**marketing plan** Describing your likely customers and how you'll sell to them.

**media** Newspapers, TV, radio and the Internet.

**milliner** Someone who makes women's hats.

**network** A group which is linked together.

**outlets** Anywhere customers buy your products.

**potential market** A place or group where you are likely to find customers.

**primary research** Finding new information that is collected for the first time.

**priority** The thing(s) that you must do first.

**profit** The amount of money you receive for sales, less the cost of making them.

**prototype** The original example of your design.

**public relations (PR)** The work you do to give yourself a good reputation.

**quality control** Checking every part of your product is as good as it should be.

**sales figures** The total amount of sales reported regularly.

**secondary research** Finding information that already exists.

**start-up** The process of getting your business going.

**strategy** The complete thinking behind the plan to make your business successful.

**sustainable** Something that can be done for a long time.

**take it public** Invite members of the general public to buy shares in your business (which means you lose control).

**target market** The people you want to interest in buying your products.

# Further information

## Websites of featured entrepreneurs

American Apparel **www.americanapparel.net/**
Chapar **www.thechapar.com**
Fifth & Brannan **http://shop.fifthandbrannan.com/**
Johnny Cupcakes **www.johnnycupcakes.com/**
Lora Leedham **www.loraleedham.co.uk/**
Masala Tee **www.masalateeboutique.com/**
Mich Dulce **www.michdulce.com/**
Missy La La's **www.missylalasboutique.co.uk/**
ModCloth **www.modcloth.com/**

Mythic **www.mythicstyle.com/**
Paperfeet **www.tombologoods.com**
Péro **http://pero.co.in/index.html**
Pinzat **www.pinzat.org/**
Prodiga **www.prodiga.co.uk/**
Ralph Lauren **www.ralphlauren.com**
Send the Trend **www.sendthetrend.com/**
TOMS **www.toms.co.uk/**

## Other websites

**www.bbc.co.uk/dragonsden/**
Official website of the *Dragons' Den* programme where you can see other budding entrepreneurs and the advice they receive.

**www.bbc.co.uk/youngapprentice**
Official website of *The Young Apprentice* series, where kids try out their skills to succeed in business.

**www.youngentrepreneur.com/**
Online forum for information and advice on being a young entrepreneur.

## Books

*Built for Success: The Story of eBay* by Aaron Frisch (Franklin Watts, 2013)
*Celeb: Entrepreneurs* by Geoff Barker (Franklin Watts, 2011)

**Note to parents and teachers:** every effort has been made by the publishers to ensure that these websites are suitable for children, and that they contain no inappropriate or offensive material. However, because of the nature of the Internet, it is impossible to guarantee that the contents of these sites will not be altered.

# Index